My Favorite BOOK

A Book About Doing Your Best & Being Your Best

This is
My Favorite Book

Please place
your school
photograph
here.

This is the way I look.
I am ____ years old.

This is the way I write my name.

_____

What is the name of your school?

_____

What is your teacher's name?

_____

What is the name of your town?

_____

What is the name of your state?

_____

Thank You!

Acknowledgments

(The people who helped make **My Favorite Book**)

My Favorite Book was written by John Sydney Tighe and illustrated by Chris Pelicano

Chris Lynch helped produce **My Favorite Book** and Chris Pelicano designed the pages.

Barbara Ferreri composed the song *Words Can Be Beautiful* especially for **My Favorite Book.**

Dedication

My Favorite Book is dedicated to the classroom educators of our children, often the unsung heroes and heroines of our children's lives. We are especially grateful to the many dedicated elementary grade teachers who have consulted with us on the writing and design of this volume as well as to the members of the American School Counselor Association. Our volume is also dedicated to parents and guardians who sacrifice each day so that their children may live the values contained in **My Favorite Book**. We also dedicate **My Favorite Book** to the generous local sponsors of the Character Program, men and women of character themselves, who care deeply for their community. And finally, **My Favorite Book** is dedicated to children in their first years of reading, may this volume represent a life long quest for knowledge and the positive character traits we hope will accompany them throughout life.

The Ambassador Company
Copyright ©2015 All rights reserved.

Printed in Korea
Edition: 5   12/2015

My Favorite Book

sponsored by

Do Your Best and Be Your Best

My Favorite Book is the Way to Go

I want to be friendly
and responsible too
and show good manners
at home and at school.

I want to make good choices
and be caring and good,
to help others in need
like I know I should.

I want to love my family
and community too
and choose everyday
the right things to do.

I want to learn all I can
that will help me to grow.
So this wonderful book
is the best way to go.

My favorite book too
it might just become.
We can read it together
and join in the fun!

Contents

See if you can find the **Be-Good Bug** in every story.

Good Manners!
About being polite and respectful of others

Words Can Be Beautiful!
About learning to read and beautiful music, too!

Being Responsible
About grandparents, good food from farms and doing our chores

Friendship
About bullies and what it takes to be a real friend

My Town
About good communities and the people who live in them

The Hero
About a kid who knows emergency procedures and does the right thing even though he is afraid

Family
About family, heritage, tradition and love

Trouble!
About poison and how Tommy got into trouble by not following the rules

Be Good to Your Body
About taking care of your body and staying healthy

Parent Guide
About helping the whole family enjoy *My Favorite Book* and thanking the people who gave it to you

Good Manners!

Being polite is simple to do, it is kindly, and respectful, and sometimes fun too!

Hello!
I'm Sherri and I am pleased to meet you.

People say I have good manners because I say "please" and "thank you" and I am polite to others.

My friends and I show good manners when we listen to the grown-ups in charge and follow their rules.

We show our manners, too, when we arrive to class on time. That is called being prompt. We respect our parents, our teachers, and any of the adults in charge who take care of us.

We learn good manners at home and at school, like being nice to our brothers and sisters and paying attention to what our teachers tell us.

We want good manners so we work at it every day! You know, good manners can actually be fun!

Hey Kids!
What do you think?

Be-Good Bug wants you to write your answers to the questions below.

About Good Manners

Here are the names of some of the people I am polite to everyday…

_____

Be respectful to your family, to friends, to children, to adults ... be polite to everyone!

When I am polite I say…

_____

_____

Words to spell:

p-o-l-i-t-e _____

m-a-n-n-e-r-s _____

Show everyone you have good manners!

Words Can Be Beautiful!

About learning to read and beautiful music, too!

Learning to read is lots of fun.
We are learning our lettters one by one.
Each letter has a sound,
and sounds are the keys.

They unlock the door to our ABC's.
Words can be beautiful, don't you agree?
I like CAT and YES and YOU and ME.

"Words Can Be Beautiful"

Composed by Barbara Ferreri

Merrily

Learn - ing to read is lots of fun,———
Let - ters have sounds and sounds are keys un –

Learn - ing our let – ters one by one,
lock - ing the door to our A B C's,

REFRAIN

Words can be beau - ti - ful, don't you a - gree?
Words can be beau - ti - ful, don't you a - gree?

I like "CAT" and "YES" and "SEE".
I like "THEM" and "YOU" and "ME".

 Can you play this song on the piano?

A Musical Matching Game

Draw a line from the name of the instrument to the correct picture.

Tambourine

Drum

Flute

Trumpet

Piano

Guitar

Tuba

Harmonica

Violin

You can visit **myfavoritebookland.com** to hear
these musical instruments and play other fun games, too.

Being Responsible

When doing a chore always do your best, then you can take a well deserved rest.

Hi! I'm Shannon. Last summer I visited my grandparents. They live in the country, and it is so much fun being with them! I love it when my grandparents tell me stories of things that happened a long time ago.

Grandma and Grandpa told me that farmers feed the whole world and work very hard at what they do. My grandparents still grow a lot of food, like corn, beans, tomatoes and squash.

They also told me that I was very responsible because I did my chores every day. I fed the chickens and I helped Grandpa clean out the barn. Now I just have to remember to do my chores at home, too! Do you have any chores to do?

Being Responsible

We should all take care of the pets we have
and keep our rooms clean, too.
What other chores around the house
are you ever asked to do?

Being responsible is not always so fun.
Sometimes it doesn't even seem fair!
But the feeling I have when my chores are all done
is such a great feeling to share!

A Story About Friendship

*Friends are not bullies, not pushy or rude.
They love to smile and have a great attitude!*

My name is Kim and I have many friends. We like each other a lot! Teacher says that friends help each other.

One time a boy in second grade was mean to my friend, Anthony. He pushed my friend and said bad things so I told our teacher. That boy was being a bully and being a bully is never the right thing to be. And it is NEVER friendly!

The Better 🐝 Way

Why does the bully here at our school
tease us all the time?
He used to be friendly and fun.
He used to be good and kind.

If this boy could see my friends and me
when we laugh and play and pretend
he might just want to join us
and become our newest friend!

Something must have happened
because he turned angry and loud
like firecrackers popping
or a dark, scary cloud!

Someone I hope will help him
see there's a better way
"I like you a whole lot better now!"
That is what I'll say!

I don't know what's wrong
when kids start to do mean things.
Inside they must be lonely
like they forgot what being friendly means.

7 Rules
For Being A Friend

1. Friends help each other.

2. Friends like to have fun with each other.

3. Sometimes friends get angry but they always make up.

4. Friends tell each other the truth.

5. Making fun of someone is not very friendly!

6. You cannot be a friend and a bully at the same time!

7. Always treat your friends the way you would like to be treated.

Make friends by being friendly!

My Town

In my town there are
lots of fun places
that make our
community great
like our school,
our firehouse and
the big red barn
up the hill on
Old Route 8.

Grandpa says people
really make our town.
They make it
a safe place, too.
Old and young, they
are friendly and kind.
We help each other,
that's what we do!

Look at the signs
above every door
and read aloud
what they say.
Did you know that
behind every single
sign are people who
work hard every day?

We like our town
lively and bright
and clean
so we all recycle
to keep it nice
and green!

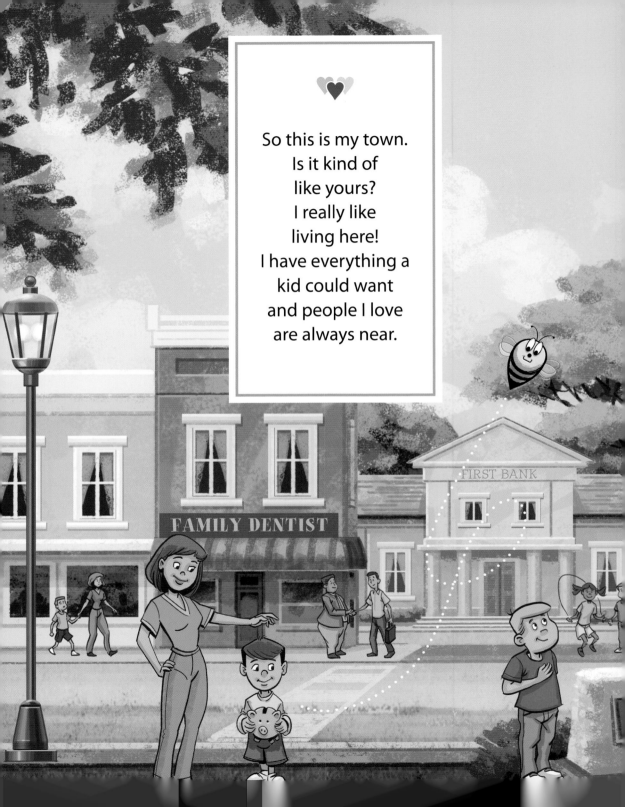

So this is my town.
Is it kind of
like yours?
I really like
living here!
I have everything a
kid could want
and people I love
are always near.

The Hero!

If you know what to do, you can be brave too!

One day when Mom was at the store
we had an emergency and I was never scared more!
My dad had an accident mowing the yard.
He fell on the sidewalk and hit his head hard.

I called 911 as fast as I could
and gave the lady my address like I knew I should.
She asked if we had any neighbors at home.
So I ran next door and got Mrs. Jerome.

I felt better when I saw the ambulance had come.
They said dad would be fine because of 911.
To know how to make an emergency call
is one of the best things to know, one of the best of all!

I was a "hero" the newspaper said
but I hadn't fed my dog, Jack, or made up my bed.
I asked Mom if her hero could watch a cartoon.
She said not until her hero cleaned up his room!

Hey Kids!

What do you think?

Be-Good Bug wants you to write your answers to the questions below.

About Being Brave

Being brave is doing the right thing even when you are afraid.

I am being brave when I …

_____

I make an emergency phone call by touching these numbers … _____

My address is …

_____

Words to spell:

       b-r-a-v-e   h-e-r-o

_____   _____

Doing what is right makes you a hero!

Family

We all have families like so many others
with aunts and uncles and sisters and brothers.
Some families combine to make one that's new.
They spread their love…that's what they do!

Sometimes in families we're clumsy we know.
But problems come and problems go!
And we always love our families even when we get mad…
when we're happy or proud or frustrated or sad.

One thing my grammy always mentions
is how much we love our family traditions.
Some traditions come from far away
like Ireland or Italy or Paraguay.
Our ancestors journeyed here long ago
from Korea or Kenya or Mexico.

Some families are large and some are small.
Some are short and some are tall.
Some are a bunch and some are a few.
Some are old and some brand new.

Each one of us is special in our very own way
like my brother whom I play with everyday.
We all have our gifts and my brother, too.
Our families see our gifts in all that we do!

Trouble!

Though sometimes it's not easy to do, following the rules is best for you!

Hi! My name is Tommy. I got in a lot of trouble after school one day. I felt really bad about what I had done!

I took out some bottles under our kitchen sink. I showed the bottles to my little sister. Those bottles are poison! The stuff in the bottles cleans our floors and our windows. If you swallowed some of it, it would hurt you!

It is against our rules to play with things like that. If I don't follow the rules Mom may not let me play on my soccer team!

Rules can keep us safe. When I break the rules or make a bad choice, it can hurt me. It is a bad choice for kids to use tobacco or alcohol. Their bodies are not going to be healthy if they do!

Hey Kids!
What do you think?

Be-Good Bug wants you to write your answers to the questions below.

About Following Rules

Rules are directions our parents or teachers or other grown-ups give us. Rules keep us safe.

Can you name a rule that keeps you safe?
_____

Can you name a rule that grown-ups follow?
_____

Words to spell:

r-u-l-e-s _____

p-o-i-s-o-n _____

Follow the rules at home and at school !

Let's Be Safe on Computers and Phones

- It is ALWAYS right to tell Teacher or Mom or Dad when I don't understand something on the computer or on a cell phone, especially ANYTHING on the internet that makes me feel bad or that confuses me.

- It is NEVER good to share ANY information about myself on the internet or on a phone unless Mom or Dad or Teacher says it is O.K.

- It is NEVER right to meet a stranger in person from the internet.

- It is ALWAYS right to let my parents know what I am looking at on the internet.

- It is NEVER good to be mean or rude or try to bully someone on the internet or on a cell phone. It is just as wrong as being that way in person and being a bully is NEVER right!

🐝 Be Good to Your Body

I like my hands and I like my feet
but when my nose stops up I can't fall asleep!
We go see the doctor if my cold gets bad
because colds can make you stuffy and sad.

My fingers work fine when they point or write
but sometimes they spill everything in sight!
Mom says don't worry, young fingers get better.
Hers help me with my alphabet letters!

Sometimes I hear growls down deep in my tummy.
So I feed it good snacks until it stops acting funny.
Our school nurse says to brush your teeth and exercise a whole bunch too!
She says if you're good to your body your body will be good to you!

A Family Guide to My Favorite Book

Good Manners

Character begins with good manners and the key to good manners is respect. Respecting others is the beginning of civilized behavior. This story points out that simple good manners mean respect for others.

Values: Respect for others, using basic good manners

Suggested Family Topic: Talk about how you show respect for others in your daily life.

Words Can Be Beautiful!

Learning to read is the beginning of a lifelong journey not only with language and the music that goes with it, but also with the ideas behind the words. This section points out that learning to read is a joyful, fun activity and that there is a wonderful connection between words and music.

Values: The importance of learning to read and the joy that the presence of music in our lives can bring to us all

Suggested Family Topic: It might be good to share with your child what kinds of books, other published materials or online reading you enjoy. If there are illiterate members of the family or that you know in the community this might be a good time to reinforce the idea that there is no shame in not knowing how to read but that it makes things very difficult for those who can't. Also, if there are any musical instruments in the home, this is the time to bring them out and dust them off! Try singing the *Words Can Be Beautiful* song together.

Being Responsible

It is important to honor our elders and to show them respect. In *Being Responsible* we also demonstrate the importance of a respect for nature by connecting the work that farmers do with our being able to have food to eat. We also connect simple daily chores with responsibility.

Values: Responsibility, respect for the natural world, respect for elders

Suggested Family Topic: Talk about some of your responsibilities. Discuss the role of your children's grandparents in your life and in their lives.

The Hero

A boy's bravery and knowledge of emergency procedures demonstrates the value of help within the community. Our reliance upon the local community is reinforced by the very method of distribution of *My Favorite Book,* that is, through the generosity of local sponsors.

Values: Bravery, responsibility, and knowledge of emergency procedures

Suggested Family Topic: Talk about people in the community who have helped your family. Use this time to thank the sponsors of *My Favorite Book.*

Friends

How we define true friendship for children is an issue that will be more and more important as time goes on. It also important to begin to address the issue of bullying. We have posted *7 Rules for Being a Friend* to reinforce the positive values in friendship.

Values: Understanding the importance of true friendship

Suggested Family Topic: Talk about one of your best friends and what that relationship means to you. Talk about your experiences with bullies.